MOVIE HITS

FOR VIOLIN DUET

Arranged by Michelle Hynson

ISBN 978-1-5400-6069-3

HAL•LEONARD®

Visit Hal Leonard Online at
www.halleonard.com

Contact us:
Hal Leonard
7777 West Bluemound Road
Milwaukee, WI 53213
Email: info@halleonard.com

In Europe, contact:
Hal Leonard Europe Limited
42 Wigmore Street
Marylebone, London, W1U 2RN
Email: info@halleonardeurope.com

In Australia, contact:
Hal Leonard Australia Pty. Ltd.
4 Lentara Court
Cheltenham, Victoria, 3192 Australia
Email: info@halleonard.com.au

ALWAYS REMEMBER US THIS WAY

from A STAR IS BORN

VIOLIN

Words and Music by STEFANI GERMANOTTA,
HILLARY LINDSEY, NATALIE HEMBY
and LORI McKENNA

Moderate Ballad

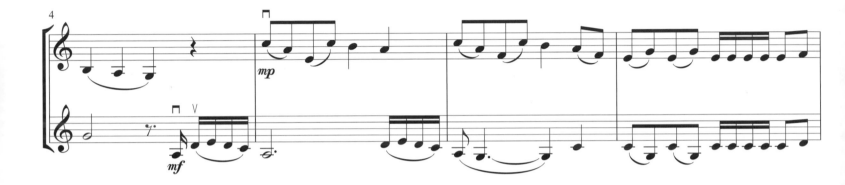

AUDITION
(The Fools Who Dream)
from LA LA LAND

VIOLIN

Music by JUSTIN HURWITZ
Lyrics by BENJ PASEK
& JUSTIN PAUL

BELLE
from BEAUTY AND THE BEAST

VIOLIN

Music by ALAN MENKEN
Lyrics by HOWARD ASHMAN

Moderately fast

THE CANDY MAN
from WILLY WONKA AND THE CHOCOLATE FACTORY

VIOLIN

Words and Music by LESLIE BRICUSSE
and ANTHONY NEWLEY

CITY OF STARS
from LA LA LAND

VIOLIN

Music by JUSTIN HURWITZ
Lyrics by BENJ PASEK
& JUSTIN PAUL

A COVER IS NOT THE BOOK

from MARY POPPINS RETURNS

VIOLIN

Music by MARC SHAIMAN
Lyrics by SCOTT WITTMAN
and MARC SHAIMAN

DANCING QUEEN

featured in MAMMA MIA!

VIOLIN

Words and Music by BENNY ANDERSSON,
BJÖRN ULVAEUS and STIG ANDERSON

THE DREAME
from the film SENSE AND SENSIBILITY

VIOLIN

by PATRICK DOYLE

FALLING SLOWLY

from the Motion Picture ONCE

VIOLIN

Words and Music by GLEN HANSARD
and MARKETA IRGLOVA

HOW DOES A MOMENT LAST FOREVER

from BEAUTY AND THE BEAST

VIOLIN

Music by ALAN MENKEN
Lyrics by TIM RICE

I DREAMED A DREAM
from LES MISÉRABLES

VIOLIN

Music by CLAUDE-MICHEL SCHÖNBERG
Lyrics by ALAIN BOUBLIL,
JEAN-MARC NATEL and HERBERT KRETZMER

IT MIGHT BE YOU
Theme from TOOTSIE

VIOLIN

Words by ALAN and MARILYN BERGMAN
Music by DAVE GRUSIN

LAVA
from LAVA

VIOLIN

Music and Lyrics by
JAMES FORD MURPHY

Easy half-time feel

MAMMA MIA

from MAMMA MIA!

VIOLIN

Words and Music by BENNY ANDERSSON,
BJÖRN ULVAEUS and STIG ANDERSON

MIA & SEBASTIAN'S THEME

from LA LA LAND

VIOLIN

Music by JUSTIN HURWITZ

A MILLION DREAMS
from THE GREATEST SHOWMAN

VIOLIN

Words and Music by BENJ PASEK
and JUSTIN PAUL

OLD TIME ROCK & ROLL

featured in RISKY BUSINESS

VIOLIN

Words and Music by GEORGE JACKSON
and THOMAS E. JONES III

THE PLACE WHERE LOST THINGS GO

from MARY POPPINS RETURNS

VIOLIN

Music by MARC SHAIMAN
Lyrics by SCOTT WITTMAN and MARC SHAIMAN

REMEMBER ME
(Ernesto de la Cruz)
from COCO

VIOLIN

Words and Music by KRISTEN ANDERSON-LOPEZ
and ROBERT LOPEZ

Moderately fast

SHALLOW
from A STAR IS BORN

VIOLIN

Words and Music by STEFANI GERMANOTTA,
MARK RONSON, ANDREW WYATT
and ANTHONY ROSSOMANDO

SINGIN' IN THE RAIN

from SINGIN' IN THE RAIN

VIOLIN

Lyric by ARTHUR FREED
Music by NACIO HERB BROWN

SOMEWHERE IN MY MEMORY

from the Twentieth Century Fox Motion Picture HOME ALONE

VIOLIN

Words by LESLIE BRICUSSE
Music by JOHN WILLIAMS

SOMEWHERE, MY LOVE

Lara's Theme from DOCTOR ZHIVAGO

VIOLIN

Lyric by PAUL FRANCIS WEBSTER
Music by MAURICE JARRE

STAR TREK® THE MOTION PICTURE

Theme from the Paramount Picture STAR TREK: THE MOTION PICTURE

VIOLIN

Music by JERRY GOLDSMITH

STAR WARS
(Main Theme)
from STAR WARS: A NEW HOPE

VIOLIN

Music by JOHN WILLIAMS

SUDDENLY
from LES MISÉRABLES

VIOLIN

Music by CLAUDE-MICHEL SCHÖNBERG
Lyrics by HERBERT KRETZMER and ALAIN BOUBLIL

THAT'S AMORÉ
(That's Love)
featured in the Motion Picture MOONSTRUCK

VIOLIN

Words by JACK BROOKS
Music by HARRY WARREN

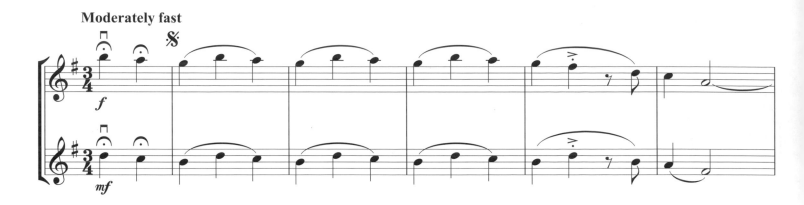

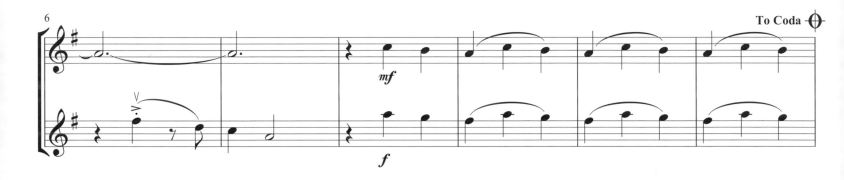

THIS IS ME
from THE GREATEST SHOWMAN

VIOLIN

Words and Music by BENJ PASEK
and JUSTIN PAUL

TOMORROW
from the Musical Production ANNIE

VIOLIN

Lyric by MARTIN CHARNIN
Music by CHARLES STROUSE

YOU'VE GOT A FRIEND IN ME

from TOY STORY

VIOLIN

Music and Lyrics by
RANDY NEWMAN

VIOLIN DUET
COLLECTIONS

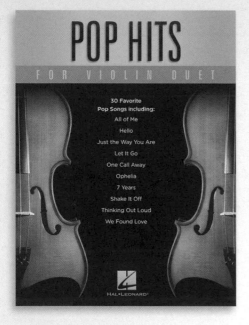

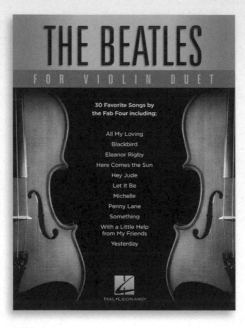

These collections are designed for violinists familiar with first position and comfortable reading basic rhythms. Each two-page arrangement includes a violin 1 and violin 2 part, with each taking a turn at playing the melody for a fun and challenging ensemble experience.

ALL-TIME POPULAR SONGS FOR VIOLIN DUET

Billie Jean • Bridge over Troubled Water • Can You Feel the Love Tonight • Hallelujah • Imagine • Over the Rainbow • Unchained Melody • What a Wonderful World • With or Without You • Your Song and more.

00222449 . . . . $12.99

THE BEATLES FOR VIOLIN DUET

All My Loving • Blackbird • Eleanor Rigby • A Hard Day's Night • Hey Jude • Let It Be • Michelle • Ob-La-Di, Ob-La-Da • Something • When I'm Sixty-Four • Yesterday and more.

00218245 . . . . $12.99

POP HITS FOR VIOLIN DUET

All of Me • Hello • Just the Way You Are • Let It Go • Love Yourself • Ophelia • Riptide • Say Something • Shake It Off • Story of My Life • Take Me to Church • Thinking Out Loud • Wake Me Up! and more.

00217577 . . . . $12.99

DISNEY SONGS FOR VIOLIN DUET

Beauty and the Beast • Can You Feel the Love Tonight • Colors of the Wind • Do You Want to Build a Snowman? • Hakuna Matata • How Far I'll Go • I'm Wishing • Let It Go • Some Day My Prince Will Come • A Spoonful of Sugar • Under the Sea • When She Loved Me • A Whole New World and more.

00217578 . . . . $12.99

www.halleonard.com

Prices, contents, and availability subject to change without notice.